Dealing With Waste

LEFTOVER FOOD

Sally Morgan

Smart Apple Media

This book has been published in cooperation with Franklin Watts.

Editor: Rachel Minay, Designer: Brenda Cole, Picture research: Morgan Interactive Ltd., Consultant: Graham Williams

Picture credits:
The publishers would like to thank the following for reproducing these photographs:
Alamy 11 (Jim West), 22 (Mark Boulton); Brand X/Imagestate 10; Ecoscene front cover top right (Kevin King), 6 (Sally Morgan), 7 (Christine Osborne), 8 (Sally Morgan), 9 (Christine Osborne), 12 (Jamie Harron), 13 (Tom Ennis), 14 (Sally Morgan), 15 (Alan Towse), 16 (Robert Pickett), 17 (Christine Osborne), 18 (Sally Morgan), 19 (Alan Towse), 20 (Christine Osborne), 21 (Sally Morgan); Kari Erik Marttila Photography front cover bottom right (Kari Marttila); Recyclenow.com front cover main image.

Published in the United States by Smart Apple Media
2140 Howard Drive West, North Mankato, Minnesota 56003

Library of Congress Cataloging-in-Publication Data

Morgan, Sally.
Leftover food / by Sally Morgan.
p. cm. — (Dealing with waste)
Includes index.
ISBN-13: 978-1-59920-009-5
1. Agricultural wastes—Environmental aspects. I. Title.

TD930.M67 2007
363.72'88—dc22   2006035137

9 8 7 6 5 4 3 2 1

Contents

Food for all

There are more than six billion people living on Earth, and the number is increasing every day. By 2025, there may be as many as eight and a half billion people. All these people need food. However, the world's food supply is not shared equally.

Shops full of food

In developed countries, there is plenty of food. Stores are full of food from all over the world, and food is much cheaper than ever before. There is also lots of food waste, as people eat what they want and throw away the rest. Much of the food is wrapped in packaging, which creates even more waste.

There are plenty of fruits and vegetables for sale at this floating market outside Bangkok, Thailand.

Going hungry

In contrast, many developing countries cannot grow enough food, so it is in short supply. The shelves in the stores are empty, and people often rely on food provided by aid agencies and charities to feed their families.

Did you know . . .

Every single day about 25,000 people die from a lack of food or some other hunger-related cause. Sadly, three out of four of all these deaths are children under five years old.

These villagers live in an extremely dry area of Ethiopia. They are preparing the ground to sow their seeds. However, if the rains do not come, the crops will fail.

It's my world!

Think about how much food you eat each day. Do you throw any away? Sometimes food travels many miles from the place it is grown to where it is eaten. Look at the labels on the food you eat. Where did it come from?

Did you know . . .

As much as one-third of the food produced in some developed countries is thrown away.

Wasting food

Look in your garbage can. How much of the garbage is food or food packaging? On average, as much as 35 percent of household garbage comes from the kitchen or garden.

These tomatoes have been dumped beside a road on the island of Tenerife. There is nothing wrong with them, but the farmer cannot sell them, so he has thrown them away.

Why is food thrown away?

People throw away food for many different reasons. Food is left on plates, in packaging, or it is thrown away because it is not wanted or liked. Sometimes food gets moldy and is no longer fit to be eaten. Sometimes food is thrown away because it is past its "use-by" date and may be unsafe to eat. Farmers, stores, and supermarkets throw away food that they have been unable to sell.

Food waste has been left on this street in Bali. If the waste is not cleared away, it could attract rats and other animals that carry disease.

Food poisoning

Sometimes it is important to throw away food that is past its use-by date, especially fresh foods, such as meat, dairy, and produce. If these foods are kept too long or not stored properly, microorganisms such as bacteria and fungi grow on them, and the foods go bad. Some bacteria are harmful and can cause food poisoning. This causes people to be very ill with vomiting and a severe stomach ache. Foods must be cooked properly, especially eggs, chicken, and food that has previously been frozen. If these foods are not cooked properly, the harmful bacteria survive and may cause food poisoning.

Stores and restaurants

Homes produce food as waste, but so do schools, hospitals, offices, hotels, and restaurants. Stores that sell food and places that manufacture processed food also create lots of food waste.

This center for homeless people uses food that has been rejected by manufacturers and makes meals for homeless and needy people. All of the food is safe to eat.

Food manufacturers

Waste is created at every stage in the food manufacturing process. Raw materials are checked to see that they are in good condition, and any damaged or moldy food is thrown away. During manufacturing, there may be misshaped or burned food. At each stage, people check the food, remove poor-quality items, and throw them away.

Waste from stores

Stores must be very careful that they do not sell food that has passed its sell-by date. They must go through the food on their shelves and check the dates regularly. Sometimes they encourage shoppers to buy food that is approaching its sell-by date by reducing the price. Food that reaches this date needs to be removed from the shelves.

This woman is sorting out food donations that will be given to needy people living in Detroit, Michigan.

Did you know . . .

Restaurants and other places that serve food can make small changes to reduce the amount of waste they produce. For example, they can use reusable plates and utensils rather than disposable ones, and they can serve sauces, salt, pepper, and sugar in large dispensers rather than individual packets. They can also use washable cloths rather than disposable ones.

Landfills and incinerators

Usually, waste food is placed in large containers or taken to landfill sites or incinerators. Landfill sites are large holes in the ground where garbage is buried. These holes are usually created by quarrying companies that dig gravel and rock from the ground. Incinerators are places where garbage is burned. Sometimes the heat from burning the garbage is used to generate electricity.

Food donations

Many supermarkets and other food businesses donate food that is past its sell-by date but before its use-by date to charities. This may include canned food and boxes of cereal. These charities give the food to the needy. Sometimes the food is sent overseas as emergency aid to feed people after natural disasters such as tsunamis and earthquakes. Food donations help to reduce the amount of food that is burned or ends up in landfill sites.

Attracting pests

Many kinds of animals are attracted to food waste.
If food is left in garbage cans, or simply put in plastic bags
on the ground, it is soon discovered by animals.

Urban animals

Rats and mice are often the first to find food waste, but large animals, such as foxes and even badgers, look for food waste, too. Animals that live in urban areas have learned that food is often left on the streets and have come to rely on it as a source of food. Foxes and badgers turn over garbage cans and rip open bags in their search, emptying garbage over the street, while rats and mice gnaw holes in bags. Birds such as gulls, crows, and ravens also feed on scraps of food on the street.

Did you know . . .

New York is trying to reduce the number of rats in the city. It is estimated that there are as many as eight rats for every person living in the city, which means a massive 64 million rats total. In the year 2000, more than $13 million was spent trying to exterminate the rats. Less waste on the streets could mean fewer rats.

Bears, such as this American black bear, are a common sight in many parts of North America around waste dumps, where they search through the bags of garbage looking for food.

The large quantities of food that are thrown away attract huge flocks of gulls to landfill sites.

Flies and cockroaches

Flies are attracted to garbage, too. They gather around landfills and garbage cans on the street and come into kitchens and factories. They lay their eggs on the waste food, and the eggs hatch into maggots. The maggots feed on the food, and within a few days, they develop and turn into adult flies.

Flies land on many kinds of surfaces such as animal droppings and garbage, so they may carry bacteria that cause disease. All food preparation areas have to be protected from flies.

Cockroaches emerge at night to feed on food crumbs on the floor. They like warm, humid places such as kitchens and cellars.

It's my world!

How clean is your kitchen? Are there any food crumbs on the floor or inside cupboards that could attract pests? Look behind your oven and under your refrigerator. You may be surprised and horrified by the amount of food you find!

13

Composting food

Food is made up of organic matter. Organic matter is made by living organisms, and it is a material that will break down naturally. This means it is easy to recycle.

Once a fresh layer of garden waste has been tipped onto a compost heap, it is covered with a lid or an old piece of carpet. This traps in the heat given off by the decaying waste.

Compost heaps

One of the best places to dispose of food waste is on a compost heap. Here, the waste can break down and form a compost that can be used on the soil in gardens. Even paper plates and paper packaging can be put on a compost heap along with garden waste.

Compost heaps range in size from small containers in the garden to huge commercial sites that are designed to break down large volumes of food and garden waste. As the waste breaks down, it releases lots of heat. It gets hot in the middle of the compost and this kills any harmful bacteria that may be present in the food. The resulting compost is full of nutrients, which can be added to the soil to help plants grow. Compost is often sold in bags to gardeners.

Quick turnaround

Composting can take weeks or months, depending on how much air and moisture the compost receives. Also, leaves and food break down more quickly than paper plates and cardboard. If it is turned regularly and there is plenty of air, compost can be made in just 12 weeks. It takes longer to make compost in winter because the cold weather slows the process. If the compost becomes wet and slimy, it is because too much soft material, such as grass clippings and vegetable peelings, has been added. This can be overcome by adding chopped-up twigs, wood chips, and some shredded or crumpled newspaper to give the compost a better texture.

Saving money

Some supermarket chains have their own composting facilities to dispose of food waste. This is an environmentally friendly method because the nutrients are recycled rather than wasted.

The Netherlands, Austria, and Germany compost almost half of their organic waste. The United Kingdom (UK) only manages to compost about 4 percent. In the United States, just over 7 percent of the organic waste in garbage is composted.

It's my world!

What can be composted?

▸ Lawn clippings

▸ Leaves

▸ Shredded stalks and hedge clippings

▸ Cut flowers

▸ Vegetable and fruit scraps

▸ Fallen apples and other fruits

▸ Teabags, tea leaves, and coffee grounds

▸ Eggshells

▸ Newspaper

What cannot be composted?

▸ Diseased plants

▸ Plastics, glass, and other non-organic materials

▸ Cooked food including meat and fish

▸ Raw meat and fish, dairy, and eggs

▸ Some weeds, such as nettles, bindweed, and ground elder

▸ Colored, glossy paper

▸ Pet droppings

Natural recycling

Compost heaps mimic natural processes. If you walk through a forest in the fall, you will see a layer of leaves on the ground. By summer, most of these have disappeared. This is because they have been broken down.

Decomposers

Decomposers are organisms that are responsible for recycling dead animal bodies, animal droppings, and plant matter. Among the larger decomposers are earthworms, beetles, and flies. Flies lay their eggs on dead bodies, and the eggs hatch into maggots that feed on the dead bodies. The larger decomposers break up the dead matter into smaller pieces, which are food for microorganisms such as fungi and bacteria. The decomposition releases nutrients back into the soil so they can be used again by plants.

Snails eat dead and decaying vegetation on the ground. They grind up the vegetation using their rough tongue, which is called a radula.

Some leaves take longer to break down than others. You can see which leaves break down the quickest by collecting many different types of leaves, placing them in a mesh bag (such as those used to package fruits), and burying the bag in the ground. Leave the bag in the ground for several months and then dig it up. See which leaves have broken down the most.

Fungi in fall

Fungi are important decomposers. Most of them live in the ground out of sight, but they can be seen in fall when they grow above ground to form toadstools. The job of the toadstool is to produce and release millions of spores, which are carried away by the wind. When a spore lands, it grows into a new fungus.

These bracket fungi are growing on an old tree stump. They are feeding on the wood that makes the stump.

Composting with Worms

Worms are great for breaking down food waste. It is possible to buy or build compost bins that are suitable for keeping a large number of special worms.

Vermiculture

Using worms to break down waste is called vermiculture. Vermiculture is becoming more popular around the world as a means of breaking down food and animal waste.

Special compost bins are set up and filled with worms that break down the food into a compost. This can take just four weeks, so the process is much quicker than a traditional compost bin. The food waste is turned into compost that can be used in gardens. As the food is broken down, a liquid is produced. This is full of nutrients that can be used to fertilize plants.

Large-scale compost bins are built to dispose of commercial food waste. In countries such as India and Pakistan, villagers dig pits about 9.8 feet (3 m) long and 3.2 feet (1 m) deep in which they dispose of organic waste and allow the worms to break it down. The compost that is formed is used to improve soil on farms.

This compost bin is made of several layers. Food scraps are put into the top layer. As the food is broken down by the worms, a new layer is added, and compost is removed from the bottom one.

Worms do not like the light, so they can be found about an inch below the surface of the compost where it is warm, damp, and dark.

Did you know . . .

The benefits of a compost bin are:

▸ less food waste remains in the garbage

▸ it is ideal for people with small gardens

▸ it produces a liquid fertilizer for house and garden plants

▸ the compost that is left behind is great for putting on soil

Hungry worms

Compost bins use a special type of worm that is smaller than the common earthworm you find in the garden. They are called red wigglers, and they are small red worms that have an enormous appetite. Some worms are able to eat their own weight in food each day. Red wigglers grow quickly, reaching an adult length of about 3 inches (7 cm) in just six weeks or less. They can live for up to two years.

Food for animals

In many parts of the world, families living in rural areas keep animals. The animals supply them with a source of milk, meat, and eggs. Food waste can be fed to the animals.

Recycling food

Food waste can be recycled if it is fed to animals such as chickens and pigs. Chickens eat a variety of foods and will peck over food from the kitchen, as well as fallen fruit and misshaped vegetables. Food waste from stores and food manufacturers can be sent to farms as animal food, too. For example, local bakeries often have arrangements with local farmers who collect all of the stale bread and feed it to pigs and poultry. However, the food should not contain any meat. Animals are not allowed to eat meat products in case diseases such as foot-and-mouth disease (FMD) or mad cow disease would get transmitted from one animal to another.

Chickens are a common sight on farms all around the world, such as this one in Ghana. Chickens provide the farmer with a supply of eggs and meat.

Pigs will eat almost all types of plants and happily feed on vegetable scraps from the kitchen or garden.

It's my world!

Some food waste is safe to put out for wild birds. Leftovers that you can put on a bird table include:

▶ stale bread

▶ cookies and stale cake

▶ fat from meat

▶ leftover cereals

▶ bruised apples

Processing waste food

There are problems with feeding waste food to animals because the content of the waste varies a lot from day to day, and this is not good for the animals. To overcome this, waste food is processed into small pellets that can be fed to animals. The nutrient content of the pellets is easier to control, and farmers can weigh out a certain amount of food each day. During the process of making the pellets, the food is heated to high temperatures, killing any bacteria that could harm the animals.

Food into new products

Food-processing factories, restaurants, and fast-food outlets use a lot of cooking oil that often ends up in drains and sewers. As the fat builds up, it can completely block a pipe. Waste fat should be recycled rather than thrown away.

Reducing oil waste

Commercial kitchens use a lot of cooking oil. This may be liquid oil or solid in the form of lard or margarine. Commercial kitchens can reduce the amount of oil they use in a number of ways, which reduces the amount of waste. Cooking oil that is used for deep-fat frying does not need to be replaced after it has been used once. Often, it can be reused a few times before it needs to be replaced. Any oil that must be replaced should be put in a large container so that it can be collected and recycled. It should not be poured down the drain!

It's my world!

How much cooking oil does your family use? A lot of cooking oil must be used in deep-fat fryers. If your family uses a deep-fat fryer, ask how often the oil is replaced. You can make the oil last longer by draining the oil through a piece of kitchen paper to remove any bits of food.

What do you do with the old cooking oil? Oil should not be poured down the drain because it could block pipes. Small quantities of oil can be mixed into a compost heap. Large quantities should be placed in an old plastic bottle and placed in the garbage.

Some recycling centers have containers for used cooking oil, such as this one in the UK.

Rendering

Waste fat can be collected from places such as restaurants and factories and taken to a rendering plant. Here the oil is cleaned to remove all of the pieces of food. The different oils are mixed together and sold to other manufacturers who use it to make soap, cosmetics, and skincare products.

Did you know . . .

In some countries, such as the UK, about 110,000 tons (100,000 t) of waste oil is produced each year.

Animal additives and fuels

Oil contains a lot of energy, so some of the reclaimed oil is used as an additive for animal food. The oil in the food helps farm animals to put on weight.

There are special oil-recycling companies that convert cooking oil into a fuel for vehicles. Cooking oil is extracted from the seeds of crop plants such as canola. This means the fuel comes from a sustainable source, as the plants can be regrown each year.

These barrels contain oil that will be recycled and used again. The oil has come from a variety of industries.

Food into fuel

When organic matter such as food rots,
it releases gases such as methane. These gases
can be collected and burned as a fuel.

Biogas digesters

In many countries, household and animal waste is tipped
into a biogas digester to make a gas for cooking and
heating water. A biogas digester is an underground
chamber, often made of
concrete. Organic waste, such
as food and animal droppings,
are collected and poured into
the digester. Inside the
chamber, the organic matter
heats up, and microorganisms
break it down to produce a
gas. The gas is taken away in
pipes and stored in an above-
ground container.

On a larger scale, modern
biogas digesters can deal with
large quantities of food waste,
such as spoiled crops and
vegetables, that would
normally be dumped in a
landfill site. The gas from
these digesters is usually
burned to produce heat, which
is used to generate electricity.

Many homes in India have a small biogas
digester outside. Animal and food waste
is poured into the underground container
where it rots and produces biogas.

This is a large commercial biogas digester in Germany. The containers are built above ground. The biogas is collected and piped to local factories, where it is burned to produce heat.

It's my world!

You can see for yourself how gas is produced from decomposing food. Put a small amount of vegetable peelings in a plastic bag, and tie the plastic bag so that air cannot get out. Leave the bag outside for a week or so, and see if the peelings have produced any gas.

Electricity from food waste

Waste food can also be burned in special waste-to-energy incinerators to produce electricity. Food contains lots of energy-rich substances, such as fats and sugars. When food is burned, it releases heat. This heat can be used to make steam, which is used to turn a turbine and generate electricity.

25

The way ahead

See if you and your family can cut down on the amount of food and packaging that you throw away each week.

Don't buy too much

Does your family buy more food than is necessary? Does the food you buy often end up in the garbage? "Buy one, get one free" offers are not a good idea if your family cannot eat or store the extra food.

Young people often eat lots of snack foods such as chips. Not only are chips and similar foods unhealthy, but they come in bags that are thrown away.

Don't be greedy

In developed countries, the number of people who are overweight is growing rapidly. This is because food is readily available and fatty foods are cheap. Try not to cook more than you can eat because it will only make you overweight or end up in the garbage. Smaller portions of food are better—they are healthier and cut down on waste.

Some uneaten food can be reheated or made into new food dishes, but remember to reheat it thoroughly to kill any bacteria that may be present. Any vegetable or fruit scraps can go on a compost heap rather than in the garbage. However, leftover meat and fish should be wrapped up and thrown away because it attracts rats.

It's my world!

Why not try growing some of your own vegetables? This is a great way to reduce food waste, and it's fun, too. It cuts out all the waste created by stores, transportation, and packaging. You can grow them in your garden or even a window box. Any waste from your own vegetables can go on a compost heap, and the nutrients can be recycled back into the soil for the next crop.

Buy from markets

Much of our food is transported long distances, which uses up fuel. The food often requires extra packaging to protect it. There are now many local markets such as farmers' markets where you can buy food that has been grown locally. The food does not need to be transported very far, so less fuel is used and there is minimal packaging and waste.

Some farms have fields of fruits and vegetables where people can go to pick their own. This reduces food waste and the energy for transportation, too.

Carrots are really easy to grow. Other easy-to-grow vegetables include tomatoes, lettuce, and radishes.

Glossary

Bacteria
microscopic single-celled organisms; some can cause disease

Biodegradable
able to be broken down naturally by microorganisms such as bacteria and fungi

Compost
to break down waste to use as fertilizer; compost is a soil-like material that is full of nutrients

Decomposer
an organism, such as fungi, that causes something to break down

Developed country
a country in which most people have a high standard of living

Developing country
a country in which most people have a low standard of living and poor access to goods and services compared with people in a developed country

Fertilizer
a substance that provides plants with all the nutrients that they require

Foot-and-mouth
a disease that affects cattle, sheep, pigs, and goats and spreads quickly from one animal to another

Mad cow disease
a brain disease that occurs in cattle, also called bovine spongiform encephalopathy (BSE)

Pollution
the release of harmful materials into the environment

Recycle
to process and reuse materials in order to make new items

Reduce
to lower the amount of waste that is produced

Reuse
to use something again, either in the same way or in a different way

Sewer
a waste pipe that carries away sewage from toilets

Sustainable
a resource that can continue to be manufactured into the future without harming the environment

Turbine
a machine with blades that spin when driven by steam, gas, water, or wind

Vermiculture
the cultivation of worms to break down waste

Waste
anything that is thrown away, abandoned, or released into the environment in a way that could harm the environment

Web sites

Composting for Kids
www.sustainable.tamu.edu/slidesets/
kidscompost/cover.html
Enjoy this slide show about composting.

Composting Waste
These two Web sites give plenty of
information about composting garden waste:
www.gnb.ca/0009/0372/0003/
0001-e.asp

www.moea.state.mn.us/campaign/
compost

Earth 911
www.earth911.org/master.asp
This Web site shows a variety of national and
local U.S. recycling programs and events.

Food Scrap Management in California
www.ciwmb.ca.gov/FoodWaste/
Web site looking at how California deals with
5 million tons of food scraps each year and
ways that this can be reduced.

Food Waste Recycling
www.metrokc.gov/dnrp/swd/foodwaste/
residential/index.asp
See how food waste recycling works in a local
community.

How To Be a Gardener
www.bbc.co.uk/gardening/htbg/module7/
growing_vegetables.shtml
Web site with lots of information about
growing your own vegetables.

**United States Environmental Protection
Agency**
www.epa.gov/epaoswer/osw/citizens.htm
Web pages showing how everybody living in
the U.S. can help to reduce the amount of
waste that is produced.

This URL takes you to a page that tells you
about food: www.epa.gov/epaoswer/
non-hw/reduce/food/food.htm

**Waste Wise for Kids: Worms
Against Waste**
www.gould.edu.au/wastewise/kids/
activity_02.htm
Australian Web page that shows you how
to build your own wormery.

Index

DATE DUE
